D1234741

To That Which Ends Not Threnody

Michel Deguy

translated from the French by Robert Harvey

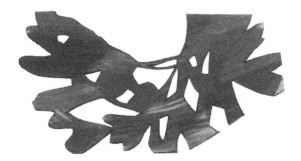

2018, nearly 2019.
for Bill & Betty.
Amitiés,
Robert

SPUYTEN DUYVIL
NEW YORK CITY

© Editions du Seuil, 1995 et 2017
Collection La Librarie du XXIe siècle, sous la direction de Maurice Olender.

Translation © 2018 Robert Harvey
ISBN 978-1-947980-56-3

cover art: Michel Canteloup

Library of Congress Cataloging-in-Publication Data

Names: Deguy, Michel, author. | Harvey, Robert, 1951- translator.
Title: To that which ends not : Threnody / Michel Deguy ; translated by
   Robert Harvey.
Other titles: A ce qui n'en finit pas. English
Description: New York City : Spuyten Duyvil, [2018]
Identifiers: LCCN 2018018751 | ISBN 9781947980563
Classification: LCC PQ2664.E45 A6413 2018 | DDC 841/.914--dc23
LC record available at https://lccn.loc.gov/2018018751

The threnody is a burial chant accompanied by dances

Outliving you isn't easy.

I believe in no afterlife beyond that which is mine, today, and whose pain resumes upon waking.

I believe in no commerce with the dead except the one I entertain with your imprint in me.

I believe in no eternal life: nowhere will we ever be reunited and sadness *consists* precisely in this sunken future that no work of mourning can fill, *this* sadness that will disappear, in turn, with "me."

A month ago my wife was dying, I cannot say you were dying, with a distressing *tu*, without addressee, and I do say "was dying," not was failing or reading or traveling or sleeping or laughing, but "was dying," as if it were a verb, as if this verb had a subject among others.

The book will be non-paginated—because each page, or almost, could be the first or the nth. Everything starts at each page; everything ends at each page.

TO MY WIFE, VANISHED INTO DEATH ON JANUARY 17TH 1994
EASTER—JULY 1994

There are thus two heartbreaks.

The second one is that of irremediable separation, following life, when love has been so altered, countered, palinodic in the course of decades, that one wonders whether it's the same.

"For the sad of heart too death has taken place."[1]

Little by little I discover, like Titus Liviticus' *quidquid progredior* on the edge of an endless ocean, the extent, of my sadness; I descend into the unfathomable, Dantesque gyration. I descend.

She has passed on; she has passed; she has passed the final ordeal. She is received by death. I descend.

And how I will reascend her past life, our life, her haunting on my back—this shred of orphic allusion—I know not. But I shall not fear turning back at her, at us, for I know that I cannot bring her back up alive.

SATURDAY, THE 5TH

It is already no longer the month of her death.

My pain is great.

My sorrow is enormous: I must write to someone, this afternoon. So, to myself. An infinite pain—overflowing its causes, which weeps not only over M.'s life, over a forlorn "me", over our life, which I'll try to describe another time; but over everything, over the whole, over the world. A flood, of tears, that would pass through my eyes, drowning. "Repetition," no doubt, of the evangelical moment, when he weeps over his fellow man, over the world, over the universe. Occasion for weeping over. *Super flumina...*

To write oneself letters: Is this a destination? Is this possible because one is alone?

I want to protect this desolation; so as to not "get my mind off it," to get in tune, to resonate with these sorry times.

Already we have gotten on to a new month.

Pietà

It's as if one were continually striking a wounded person already prone, there, on the ground, under our feet, beaten; silence has become her silence; general ignorance, her loss of consciousness. Things, like her, no longer breathe; no longer respond. Everything we do, say: so many blows, mortal, overpowering a child, beating down weakness, burying her a little more—her, the disarmed one—, without reply, the vanished, the shattered one. I no longer protect her. But did I protect her or did I reduce, evince her?

To weakness, to those who are on the bottom.

I covered the images of your agony with plaints, moans.

I put my wedding ring, our symbol, on her finger for the second time in forty years on January 17th.

At least I won't ever cause her pain again.

She was the courage of our vain condition, she who assumed tasks, and touched off laughter.

Strictly bringing the two edges together, she tucked in things imposed.

Now the abyss into which I fall with her widens into revealed sadness.

And as I no longer open or close curtains or shutters, the bedroom is in mourning—black. And when its door remains ajar, there is that dark vertical line, that narrow column of black marking the separation in the sitting room.

Might it have been possible to offer her death? I mean to hand her over to death more tenderly, looking at each other more often in and through this knowledge? in a daily approach to this death? To tenderly lay her down, to deliver her unto death as one puts a child to bed? tucking her in, caressing, caring for her in her dying [*morition*], with pain and tears left on her face? accompanying her up to

...possible if we had been older still, less modest too after all those years, more confident in a past that might have been less contentious, exchanging love for death, death with love

also, of course, if I had abandoned you less often at the threshold of churches, if praying had had meaning, but I had removed that from you as well, I had also dried up your pious soul, subtracted the

if I had been better able to speak of the things on our agenda, such as

to
go into retreat, and of suicide, and

heartrending

I must also say something of *that* love: of M. and of Rafaël, her last love, the most intense one of what will have been the last part of her life. The mere inscription of the name, the mention, the proper name of that love, the monogram MR, the plexus tightens and the whole *thumos* fills with tears, that love to the point of crying, nearly eight years, that love that I cry over today, threatened by death, asphyxiated by death, and during the final weeks she barely wanted to see him, shame had the upper hand.

I don't know if the syntagma "grandmother" which dresses up femininity with a vague infirmity, illustrates it with a heavy or undone body, a crushing stereotype, that caricature which every social class makes even worse with its euphemisms— it's *mémée* in the lower one and *mamy* in the upper—, I don't believe the syntagma with its phylactery in endless and mediocre imagination, prepares for considering that love, for treating it well, for doing it justice, that love that held sway over her and couldn't hold her because death is stronger than love.

Playtime, the first little books, prayer, the bed in the morning, the garden, crossing streets with hand held, ABCs, anxious vigilance for the least deviation, the protection, cards ("battle," "fish"), rote repetition, drawings pinned up in the kitchen, the photos, the body growing by the week, the fever watch, the endless kisses, the batches of wash, the hugs, the glass of water at night, vacations, when school lets out, protection from the rain, shade from the sun, the nicknames, washing up, dance, praise, scolding, pastries, help with grammar—Do Kamo, the grandmother-grandson couple.

Soon enough the deep sigh, that dismisses as it evokes the memory, the haunting, will come and substitute for the tears. I don't like it that ex-intimates "do their best" to not even pronounce your name, to relate a shred of the past, and everything to bury in amnesia, to bring on Lethe. "Soon enough the opposite of insomnia will come [...]"

If I don't wrap mourning in care, who will? or else it too will pass over into the future perfect. Yes, I have three lectures to prepare this week, but instead of applying myself to them, I should to you, to us. That's what mourning used to be for.

And everything that used to be at issue in the war between us identical to a thing people childishly fight over, but which one, and that now no longer interests me because it's too much wholly mine. We've left the state of indivision and its duel.

Her request was that I not leave her alone, that there be a prioritary *us*, that I not relegate her ("Oh repudiated Woman!"...). And at long last that's nevertheless what happened: disappearance, discomfiture, to such an extent that within only a very few days after the relegation to the earth, "people" no longer speak to me about her—this happened more quickly, implacably than I feared. Mourning is even more *private* than I was afraid. The horror of my irreparable injustice, of this lapse that her death renders "essential" (   ) is sealed.

A man tired of the genitive and tired
Of the story of the same divided against itself
—oh repudiated women—
Bearing the bundles of knowing
But in the shape of scythes on the field

Apostrophes on the head's temples
Beside the spotted beasts that would die to the edge[2]

I'm going to take off once again, with lots of trips for years perhaps, from now on none of these widened distances that she would fear will separate us any more than that between the window at Hauterive to the cypress in the cemetery on the horizon; infinite distance.

Or else go into retreat and meditate on all this. But I must get used to working in hotel rooms which will be no stranger than the rooms of solitude in our homes.

Did I not retire following the painless shock of 1987 to write *Le Comité*? But that was in familial bliss at the foot of the Ventoux. Give up that African or American trip to write this booklet in one sweep? Or write it in Africa...

With whom to speak?

How to grow old? How to die? Those are the questions.

"Hymen Hymeæus! You remember our wedding beneath the sulpician nave, one September 16th, Sylvie carried the train, Nicolas the orange blossom, Marie the white book."[3]

Those are the lines I wrote to her in a book of 1973, 20 years after our marriage. Or sometimes more secretly; and I'll murmur as if I were leaning toward her ear, toward her heart, the opening words of a few poems. There are so many. From the period when I wrote: "The days are not counted…".

To know why you are so dear to me

Now I shall speak a language all our own
Oh my unique wife
your pink cornea your dress for crying
you left me in the labyrinth[4]

To the point where the poem implicates
Aim I await you everywhere
(when I take care of my love
it makes fun of me)
The hydrangeas prefer the house
(For her I describe life with exactitude)

Resource of marriage
It is the visible
Blindly chosen[5]

The memory of a dress which one had put on
I won't describe it for you. Tomorrow
Like a dress which one doesn't dare put on
For a sacrament a wedding a baptism
It is folded under the black in the bed
Like the garb Bajazet in Istanbul

The beautiful day like a dress
Shed now in the shed.[6]

And many others...

Now Monique my wife is dead and the lengthy agony was not spared her, Monique the frail, the wounded, the resistant, showed us the strength, the soul. In my notebook of nearly two months ago she had written in order for me to come across it: "You must understand that for me it's incurable."

Knowledge of this, all this, from way back, fatally, and having held with her to the end with my children, my friends—I enclose relatives, beloved—in this failure to render assistance to a beloved one in the process of dying does not prepare one, prepares one for nothing. It's desolation. There's no consolation.

Tenebrarum lectio. Pulvis es et in pulverem reverteris. Verba Ecclesiastis filii David /.../ Vanitas vanitatum dixit Ecclesiastes. Vanitas vanitatum omnia vanitas.

"You have forsaken me."

The dying one is forsaken: a Gospel truth. Abandonment is tenderness in dying [*le mourir*], the rebecoming a stranger to the closest other. She has gone to that place where I hadn't known her.

The body's soul *is* immortal, yet it is abandoned along with it, as if nothingness were other and stronger than being.

I must say it's been a long time since I believed in any of this which is so magnificent, *splendor veritatis*, and my soul is sorry in this moment of saying goodbye, with you, to Monique; ...and so, many here bid her ADIEU better than I do.

Monique goes before us—slightly. There is no consolation.

Monique was just 60 years old and we lived together for 40. "For better or worse, until death do us part." Of the better my heart fortunately is filled and I should also be able to speak of the better.

As for the worse... I have learned the truth of this thought: that EVIL is the obsession with what one does not *desire*. But that each one's guilt increases with the intertwining of destinies. And it's huge.

"Love stronger than death"—What does this mean? This is the atom of reality, the articulation, the day's brittle atom, the principle of individuation, the mediating triangle, the plus-one of two, the between-them of siblings, of parents-children, of lovers, of spouses. This is the only witness that there is existence. There is none except by means of this relation that precedes the terms, that makes generations, favorites, close ones; this is the subject and not the altogether closed *individuum*, the self-preferring *auto*, the self-serving *self*, that deserted individual that terror needs to increase its reign. This is the subject, the subject of what is at stake; history is history of love—or nothing.

Time and its use have changed—since the day... Starting at seven, seven thirty, I kept an eye out down the hallway for the awakening of her suffering—and who else now besides me will carry her haunting in memory, her rhythm in mine, the care of her?

Each time perhaps
will I never see you again
Thus it is built like this: to see in order to never see each other again.

Seeing says: we will not see each other again
Life will have been like
a first last date
—to get first comparisons first.

Will ploughing through sadness allow me to penetrate some secret? That's not certain
The abyss ploughs itself; pure opportunity for discovering the extent of the disaster.

You knew you'd be vanquished
in this exhausting unequal battle
Now that the field of our struggle
and which was one of loving
is all mine, devastated.

..."Like a life that no longer makes sense," you say. And I add: there remains the meaning that a life that no longer has meaning has— in other words meaning remains.

Life made some consciousness, and consciousness made some *me*, consciousness in the "me" mode. And this me's attachment to life or should one say that of these mes and of all forms of the subject—is so strong that it will have ended up destroying life; and finality, in the end, the powerful teleological current, will have given birth to such powerful counter-finality that ends and the end of ends will have been covered over, crushed by it.

And often, coming back "from the far end" of the apartment (from my office) toward the kitchen, walking by an empty bedroom bordered by a hallway, whose door I like to leave open *in view* of what I am in the process of telling, I enter, attracted by its window for nothing other than to go to the edge of that window for nothing other than to look out, the courtyard, the street, an instant, the time of a look as one sees hurrying "people" in the street glance surreptitiously sideways into what an open *cochère* offers, simply because the *cochère* is open, and, if the wall had gone on uninterrupted, they would have passed on without a glance—out of pure curiosity, thus: this is not an "explanation"; it is—it is curiosity, hence *tautology*: on both sides of the "is"—the same. In saying "out of curiosity," I suddenly get at what curiosity is by the fact, the example, in this case, *by setting it*. That's what curiosity is and nothing else. There is curiosity, it's when; it's like when.

What comes along to attest and, in a certain sense "measure"
the meaning of the world in the sense that Jean-Luc Nancy lent the
term is our attachment to "life" whatever happens, implausible and
… insane attachment to this life of ours, the one called *ordinary*, the
common one; whatever happens, or almost, I mean with the exception
of intolerable pain that suicides some; the insane joyance of the idle
instant, whose verso is that despair of dying disproportionate to all
the reasons to take no interest in what follows and I shall name some
of these reasons (the daily botching of humanity)… to melancholy,
misanthropy, hatred, and I shall describe this joy, this pleasure alone.
Despite this knowledge: that to exist is to inexist for the appalling
multitude of others, clearing out everything around one (the opposite
of what they call God, for by God they mean the love, I suppose, that
all the others might bring, the identity of loving and one another).

As if she were alive and were *deprived* of life! Which is another superstition. That was only true of the final days of life.

"Eternally" means forever, evermore, in our life. It's the break that death introduces, permanent dematerialization, how to say it, the explosive hushed disintegration of life's halves that introduces that extreme difference, the strongest, "*quo majus nihil concipi possit,*" which is hyperbolized into "eternity." Encircled heart, shrunk by emptiness or like some Theater of Memory whose boxes, blowing up like silent personnel mines, were randomly and ceaselessly erased. Tubercular amnesia.

The book will be non-paginated—because each page, or almost, could be the first or the nth. There is no ordinal series. Everything starts at each page; everything ends at each page.

I cherished you.

"There's nothing to be done"—I was executioner only to the extent that I made this sentence my favorite one, for nothing at all for everything.

Did we forgive each other?

December 8th 1993

Michou, my love,

Of course L. didn't give you the same version he gave me only two minutes before.

The tumor is *inoperable*. He spoke with Doctors R., L., everyone agrees on palliative care, alleviating the pain so that I die peacefully. That's what I hope will happen God only knows. I try to eat every two hours; after M.'s dinner, hook up a vial to keep me going. I don't see what superhuman, subterranean forces could get me out of this 27-year bad turn. A real good c... that could have been operable like so many others have would have been better. This type is the worst and in the worst place.

Help me fight. After 24 hours of crying, I begin a new battle. Was L. the messenger of all this?—I think so; that's why he came, a bit up tight, awkward, trying to run with the hare and hunt with the hounds.

MARCH 20TH. 4:45 A.M.

It's been more than two months since we saw each other. It's the first time we've been apart for so long. And I write this, I'm not writing to you, in the agony notebook where I find, noted down by or for the nurses, the simple daily schedule, the doses of morphine (6:30 a.m. – 40; 10:45 a.m. – 40; 3:30 p.m. – 40; 7:30 p.m. – 40; 10:30 p.m. – 40…)

Already the entoptic cloths of memory, Veronica's material impregnated with your face, the whole iconography—none of this is automatically activated by the psychic machinery any more. Already the sobbing no longer bursts forth on call. The drought is beginning. There are only five or six humans who weep over you without tears every day. We've handed the thought of you over to inscriptions, the back of images, collective formulas.

I should wrap you in care; not turn away from the source at all, not listen to the clichés of distraction at all.

Oh gestures of lovers
And rhythms of their feints
Carried on long-stemmed tears
Cold lovers turn to face toward their heat
And as from a winter fire they move away insufficient[7]

I can't even tell you the truth.

After some weeks—few months but many weeks already—I
need to not "get my mind off it," to not augment the distance, to not
accumulate, confusing the path, days, screens, blockages, as when
one wants to lose an enemy who stalks us, between your deathbed
into which your lifebed had little by little changed, raft, Egyptian
boat for the tomb, with the pharmacy, the books, the newspapers,
the bedclothes, the phone, the bedpans, the cloths, the scissors, the
cotton, the syringes,
 between that bed and today, let's call this today, I need to care
for the sadness, keep watch over the mourning, to retreat with the
children, before the diminishing, before Lethe's rising [*hausse*], before
the cover [*housse*] of its clay over all the things that it took one day to
transform into memories

What to write on the stone, the rectangle of pale marble chosen this
morning in the horizontal cemetery? I'll rummage through my poems;
or this title:
 to that which ends not.

There was something in the fact of being married, each at the focus of our ellipse, which concentrated and retained, struck my dispersion, my amnesia, my prodigality, my shrugs; there was a force of synthesis, a memory; there was a home. And all this came apart and is coming apart, and defection carries me away.

I must sketch out her life with exactness, what parts courage, devotion, endurance played in it, and discouragement, resolution, limitation, permanent fear and laughter, defeat and horror.

Scarcely a few weeks now and I hesitate to go back in order to fix the entoptic face of our life and her death; of our death. If I accommodate rememoration on her face as it petrifies in my head, tears well up, a cold of the soul; the soul trickles between body and memory. Viduity.

Why struggle against death?

What I do not *desire*, truly *not* this is evil, the obsessive, says the moralist. This is what escorts me, assists me, spectral beggar, in the plural, that others don't see or hear, obscene haunting. Mr. "Hide"... How to purify?

To absorb, to reabsorb, evil, to digest its bad secretions, without dreams, without repression, I was going to say without psychology, so that evil has no *reality* (no realization), what to do? Recognize what is bad for what it is? face down the obsession of counter-desire? avow it? "express" it, as the expression goes? ingurgitate, digest, overcome it?... to be its impassive garbage chute, carrying the dejection of abjection at one's side like Pascal's abyss?

I relate that conjugal life was contentious, violent, "impossible." I suffered from marriage like no one, like many—like everyone?

And I occasionally cursed it, secretly and in private, and publicly; and wrote about it scandalously, searching for the beginnings of a novel, like here:

Before entering into this book, I, *this one* ran a bookstore in the 6th; taught, ran a restaurant, a toy store.

Where were we? We were demonstrating Fermat's theorem, we were abrogating Fallou's law, we were embarking on a big French loan. It occurred to *this one* that the 19th survived tenaciously.

This one's mistress's tummy skin was wrinkled, welted, her legs were fat, her breasts smaller than an athlete's, her face narrow and vulgar, she was sensuous and bejeweled. She read magazines, lived in an apartment made for upper management types in Parly II. And if she happened to come once in a while, it wasn't thanks to this one but by her own means, she knew what to do and while he penetrated her with the usual mediocrity she caressed herself and achieved multiple orgasms through her sensitive clitoris, skillfully coinciding with his.

The novel ensures comm-uni-cation. Monday, it's empathy; Tuesday, sympathy; Wednesday, sympathy. And Thursday? It's empathy...

Sometimes the dream hardens, becoming *religiously correct*. One purifies. The rabbi refuses his daughter's hand to the goy; the baptized girl will not marry the Hadj's son; the Roman catechist will not become the pastor's son-in-law. No marriage, no mixing! The human species is not for tomorrow.

And the long days during which she was bored... What a married man "will have desired" most often, most obsessively, is separation; frequent separations, then separation.

To take up again this S&M story, this tenuous, scientific, plausible version of things.

From now on I've pulled back, but how, from the living, turned toward the dying; engaged in being-with-them and as though half-buried.

The best is *also* alibi; perfect alibi.

Perfect alibis are alibis.

Forced by life to remain alive, forced by life to take an interest in life, in my life, which don't interest me. Forced to own up, utter, fear, desire… —to live.

"Something more interesting than life," I had written in *Au sujet de Shoah*.

All those poems that you blamed me for not having more expressly, nominally dedicated to you in the book, right on

and the other women who were not my wife complained that I didn't inscribe their names right on the book.

Shearing, beam key, a day; storm, beer in the barn, wiped moons, a day; menses refertilized five hundred times, a life; shifted haystacks, hurdles, mud clods trod, a day; market, nails that mend, coffin false heel, a day; dream, ivy, rosacea, sales, a day a month a life; mottled dogs, pastors' shortcomings, ruts, accidents, an evening, a morning, an era. Misdeeds and handkerchiefs, pride, conjugal spats, trail of leaves, a day a day a day; in a year, in six years, I'll wait I sow we will love one another [je sème on s'aimera] *boots, rain on skin, furled tarps, frenzy and servants, inheritance; wind bodily seized, rust, coronation, immortal obsolescence, yet a day; wages, smiles, cords* [fils] *held by hands to the clouds, to the trees, snap, a noontime, an evening; murder, circus, I die, tumor* [je meurs, tumeur]; *son* [fils] *don't forsake me, the animals are taken ill, I'm coming, I'll come, wait for me a day, a year; servants, hats, infrangible statutes, machines, beer; why have you forsaken me, hair* [cheveux] *and willows, horses* [chevaux], *mud, ponds, sabers, I sweat* [je sue]; *it might have been* [ç'eût pu être], *established, betrayal, bedding, neighborhood misalliance, brick slopes, debts; hardy, Dorian, stoneware* [grès], *squander, moronic, alban cliff, the past passed through the chain of the book, of film, of TV, storm here. Opulence, books, beyond remedy, the wind's tithe, bitter love veers, corsets, milk, blood; jabots, demur, common law, the wind, a day, a century, the fresco counts, do nothing, oblivion on the moors, howling wind* [hurlevent[8]], *go-between, child, tree, book, timberline, Biblical destinies; one day, one year, stele, lose; crinoline and trail, kitchen, abuse, no one knows; father, absent, thus, fog, adultery for our interviews, loss, adieus, the deceased comes back to die, America, I'll not go if you maintain your gaze.*[9]

This is the first time that I leave you without your being here. I'll no longer hear your voice, scarred for so many years, covering poorly its wound of so many more years, the voice when I phoned from afar and that as far as you were concerned it was finished forever for a few days, that spoke the injustice the abandonment against all plausibility since a few days after the course of the other injustice, the daily one, took up again, your voice without reasons, and you were right so many years in advance since in the end you would be abandoned, you will have been abandoned, you knew it, your voice asphyxiated by absence and the insane distance, and the normal, the reasonable the necessary and the insane separation, your being desiccated by the sudden, obvious, crushing fatality, the lack of being, the default of what had been promised, the failure to be together, the cruel default inflicted, victimary inflection, your being infected with proofs

and in place of unison the reciprocal, instantaneous, brutal wound of the telephone, as in an assault by vulnerable duelists, stricken, stricken simultaneously by the blunted tip of the other for the thousandth time "O rage of ripened hearts at grips with love!"[10]

This is the first time that I leave you without your being here to suffer, and instead of at least getting a reduced sentence, instead at least of not making you suffer, it's my abandonment, the one I desired, citing taciturn and constantly menaced love, that wrings the stomach's sponge and turns me into a weeper, as if the voyage aggravated for so many years by these bad conditions, this contagion of reciprocal wrongdoings, had found its system of melancholy, its tone of inevitable failure, something to feed on and give in without regret to its interruption.

I awaken on the equatorial lagoon, well before their dawn, as usual, and it's for the anniversary and its alarm, a month ago my wife was dying, I cannot say you were dying, with a distressing *tu*, without addressee, and I do say "was dying," not was failing or reading or traveling or sleeping or laughing, but "was dying," as if it were a verb, as if this verb had a subject among others.

"/the friends/with a big heart of whom you were jealous"

In the beginning Godo, Iommi, poetry in the form of outings ("*phalène*"), of the long trip ("*Améréïde*"), or of nocturnal sessions of collective translation: the time taken, the painful tension between the private, wounded by hospitality, and that public or, rather, "friendly," masculine, intelligent life that took, deprived you of affection, that deviated the course. And, at the other end of life, this repeat offense, the friendship with L., imperious, grave, afamilial, it was repetition, nocturnal kidnappings.

The friendship that she suffered and from which she might have suffered even more if I hadn't distracted her, diluted her jealousy by dint of a general infidelity that seemed to prefer everything to conjugal intimacy.

No point in attempting to mourn mourning. Under the sway of mourning thought passes (thinks) time, discontinuously but all along, measuring in everything the extent of the loss: the indivision of being and a being, the union of being and of loss, the subtraction of being from being… Death becomes the guardian angel. Perishing is perceptible.

And, in a certain way, it was the end of friendship; solitude becomes absolute in losing its interlocutor from the period of maturation, of parenthood, of transmission, of fashioning. My companion, the voice of confidence, my alterity. No one else, however tender, however caring he might be, shares the mourning. They separated.

In friendship there was some incredulity—something like a "desperate attempt": belief, in which one cannot entirely trust, that one might find it to be an overall equivalent, like something that would stand for the rest, that would balance out and compensate for the general lack of comprehension, of exchange, of communication between spirits.

And in this last part of life pardoned by mourning, she herself ignorant of its length or its shortness, and at the same time as mourning favors a duplicity that enjoys seeing ever-ready and reversible laughter and tears, warmth and frigidity to alternate, grows the need to pull oneself together, to sum up, to pass on with simplicity—what I call poetry, the thrust that consists of holding together (*sum-balleïn*) in a work of language, in the wisdom of the last quarter, the Ecclesiast's vain renunciation of vanity, Herclitus's contraries, Cervantes's enchanted disillusionment, Mallarmé's paradoxal abnegation—and the benevolence, the admiration, the safeguard, the interpretation that despoils and transports the lettered spirit into simoniac letter.

But since we can only live as if we didn't die, thoughts that wear the veil of incurable sadness do not add to truth.

Chance caused me to return to Nantes, forty years later: it had been my first "job" and our first "home." I had brought you to those halls of the Museum in Rue Clemenceau. (We were living right near the Lycée. Living with a man, and in the same bed, was hard. Troubled nights were beginning. As soon as you were pregnant you went back to your mother's.) And I find Ingres and the three Georges de La Tour again. And those great, mad "pompier" paintings one of which imagines the "Flood," milk or sperm raining down on nudities—a European flood that drowns only women and white ones, piles of entrails, soaked pity: in which is emblematized (*escutcheoned!*) in fact a sort of pure preference for the family for its intimacy, its steaming body, a kind of enormous incestuous mishmash, a gyneceum submerged by its own humidity, melting, amalgam of breasts and crotches—live chalk of steaming flesh on the paupers' grave of flesh.

And all those gouache or oil jam-jars in other halls... Critics and historians can speak of "new light" in regard to the "impressionists" only because *things* are recognizable in effigy, un-painted on the canvas: if there were only colors, even colors of light abstractly sampled and applied within the frame, one would still not *see* the new light. But there are fruits, faces, houses, fields: a de-finition of quasi-things; luminous things, and thus light.

With this sound of a regular heartbeat in our ear we ourselves are a pacing in the night. We are truly alone, on the move, and it's nighttime, with this sound of a heart beating apace.

Life is a private affair, it's a dream; reverie of the solitary one, the dream of family life, Rousseauist, errant, sporadic, original, autarchic, paradisiacal, with love at the edge of the fountain, and the Italian song before languages, one's heart on one's lips, it's a dream, life with no reason to end; no reason, thus. Flocculation of great affectionate polymeric monads, each one "alone in the world" in a world made for its happiness, with melons predisposed for being sectioned for the family. A few millennia later, the catastrophe is conjured on the edge of Clarens, or a few centuries later still on that of the Dallas dollar-filled swimming pool.

Alone in the world, or almost, give or take a few billion, that's the problem. As for the others, the other others, those living in the street, they are subjugated, ransomed, contributing to the family's homeostasis, one per neighborhood making an armistice with the other families; Sicilian style.

For them the page is turned; not for me. I turn it over. And if it be true that not only the author, not mostly, not exclusively the author, is interesting, but the character, and "Heathcliff" more than the Brontë sisters, or Lucien than Stendhal or Billy Budd than Melville, then try through the autobio to place oneself into fiction, into a character—so that at least he will be legendary, known, recognizable, interesting; that mummy, that filiation, that guy.

For them that furtive page of their memory is torn, that bookmark that they will hardly ever read again, even if they sign themselves with it sometimes; it yellowed, then was obliterated, erased, returned to dust. Not for me, of course. No acceptance.

That there was nothing else—than the fact that nothing happened, nothing but the brief encounter and that we said everything; the exchange of the interminably brief with briefly interminable; that nothing took place but this passage, this fake whole, destroyed by the knowledge that it's nothing—this is precisely what each person evokes when encountering the other: Do you remember? The rain, the mustard, her dress on that day; and everyone smiles. And it's this nothing that we miss. There's nothing that we don't miss.

You descend back to earth, you tell me, when you leave
The mountain, her serenissima highness, the *Heitere*
Of Hölderlin. Yet that was the earth as well, that most high
There are thus two on-earths on earth

There is so much time that we take it we lose it
We waste it we throw it from rooms, life
She passed through we didn't take note of her appointments
Those wounds of the soul: the ones we don't tend

Somber is life and I don't know
And I answered her I hope
That there's a heaven for the others[11]

No predicate can qualify the whole rather than its opposite. Yes,
"man" *is* ridiculous, and sometimes magnificent. Why would one win
out over the other? Or if it depended on us, on action, to cause one to
pass before the other—locally. And I wander in the unqualifiable.

If I could change something in the bloody and stupid course of the
"world"—another could too and would undoubtedly do the opposite…

Subject—of whom?

Light-years from the center, from the "sun," far from "power" like Pluto or an asteroid in a "system": each "situates himself" as such, distant, alone, miserable, "further than you"… if he has a thought for those billions of others.

At another time [*fois*] (another faith [*foi*]) *equi*distance from the center or God, creator of me-you, reigned, ruled. Now each, null, abyssally separated from the lighted stage, or center, which is a TV screen-set itself unknown to all the other TVs… with the exception of the screen of screens, or CNN, American stage standing for the chorus, worth the heavens painted for centuries with the court of the chosen damned but all chosen to be around, surrounding the Supreme Court, God King Sun; where the chances for one to be received, treated, are now slimmer than they were in the 17th century for a subject to be seen by all.

Dereliction of the modern subject.

What's there to say about the "old crazy woman" on the ground floor who says she's uneducated, empty, devoid of "inner life," stupid, in other words? She's right, and *that's* what we respect in the other: her "life," the fact that she (he) is alive that's all, that's her alterity as other, as "neighbor": we *identify* her by her freedom, and thus by absolute value, infinity.

Intelligence disarms, paralyzes *itself*. Were it to follow its interests, its logic, it would be violent. Systems that transgress the limit to which I refer, or "infancy," for "better," are fanatical, violent. Intelligence cannot make a world, the better world that it makes us understand and even wish for.

Thus, "So-and-so" was more a friend than X or Y who were so close! Two unexpected condolent lines that came from afar, trembling, will have been the mark and measure, the pathometer, of this sympathy and their silence the measure of the inverse. And the hurried error that betrays feigned concern wounds more than the indifference of routine. In contrast to *nekros* becoming *thanatos* in tragedy, the deceased of our ages is expulsed; more completely than I believed, so insufficient was my disbelief. Placed into disappearance, the departed, effaced by the inter-living. While "clearing," the rows thicken without stopping anything. It's one of the modalities of *disproportion*, one of Pascal's notions to be inherited, remediated, articulated with the recent one of the *double bind*.

Disproportion—represent this to yourself: the worst never ceasing to worsen; the catastrophe, the tidal wave in slow motion; the magnification of the wall; the thick lens of agony. And then mourning's magic trick: the disappearance of the dead person, and of death. The crime's intrigue (where did the corpse go?), that's what happens, to all of us, ceaselessly. It's intriguing. Dodging, fading, blackout, oblivion.

One's immediately on the other side; this one, the side of the living; those over there, from the gravepit, taken back into the traffic of the living, block up the difficulty of being.

The experience is of Disproportion: the catalogue spells and declines it; the analogue conjures it, desperately.

At one side the minute insects of death; at the other the ridiculous sect of consolers, the reassurers. At one side the mute harassment of death; at the other death not counting.

Scrutinize, then, this logic that speaks in *locutions*, while being said, opening up, confidentially, in those expressions reputed to be "figurative," idiomatic lexicalizations of the language, those deep vernacular syncategorems, never thematized enough, the untranslatables: everything that *the language of the mother tongue* negotiates, it's this Disproportion. And nowhere else is it heard.

Disproportion keeps any ontological thinking of Dike— conjoining—in check.

Dying-for (speed, for example; look at that motorcyclist…) and kill-for (speed, for example; what an accident!): one and the same thing.

(Hauterive)

And that office in the fields, backed up against the timberline that stares at the nape of my neck through the large bay window at its end, where I worked without a timepiece, slow crossing of the afternoon on that docked cemented barge, punctuated by your *visits*. For you were my visitor, coming from the house with a child in your arms, then by the hand; you appeared from the side facing the country. And what we didn't say, what we will have never managed to say, made up the fathomless depth of our ever lessening words, like the oceanic altitude beneath the swimmer's lazy stroke.

The frustration of her existence, which was counterbalanced only by the promise of little revelation the next day—tomorrow would be the day before—now the promise was suddenly broken, set down by the announcement of death that came in a matter of days.

It's over, murmured the night: a murmur that can be neither written nor heard—Mane-Thecel-Pharès in my head alone.

The tiny differences, a thousand and one details in which we differed, objects of familial debates of the "I like/I don't like" order, in which her choice determined the course of things, because out of two things one must be preferred and decided upon and, for example, curtains must be drawn in the evening to hide the dark and thus the style of communal existence be less the result of concessions than faithful to the manner of being of one of them, and it was hers, now its sequence is abandoned or turned upside down because I no longer draw the curtains on the dark and don't make the bed, and it's an erosion, a ruin, an infidelity, an amnesia.

Who will take care of what I'm forced to call "me"? Nobody will ever care for "me" any more. Who will like this office, be alert to its disorder, clean off the ashes? Even when things were "ours" and not mine, indivisibly, with the part and the angle that she took, this made them mine differently, possible for me. These are less mine now that they are no longer ours

Disjointed, dislocated, at a depth unsuspected (by me), I am perhaps already destroyed.

Hold this moment when she sits down
Moderating the skirt to the right to the left the eyes
The legs drifting on the tiles allowing
The fingers to find themselves again the pronominal body

On the axis where we—for we are the axis
Customary sojourn under oblong skies
Surrounded by earth There is a need for bays in the chateau
Including the networks on the walls
And the vista thanks to the lure of the gardens

As one looks out the train
Where the windows are vast and numerous
The margin of music and for colors
The temple of canvas was contrived[12]

She helps him on with his gown
And the extremity of his soul the fingers
Are careful of his arms of his body
If it were not for the detail of the body
To whom the votive soul?[13]

The other night at the zenith of my uphill street, "offered" to my careful gaze slowly raising my eyes, the moon in the anfractuosities of gray-black sky opened by the two buildings at the corner, estuary, the moon halved, at once clear, discernible and milky, fringed or cloudy, in itself cottony.

That thing, thus, like an addressee figure, as a vocative mirror for a self-portrait without reflection, forever mute and augur, that thing of inevitable superstition, which "enters my life" as into that of Leopardi or of multitudes, in relation to "me" and, at the same time, its other-being, without relation, that mineral alterity same as anything, without "disdain" since all (anthropom)orphism here, precisely, was extinguished at the very moment, that of an asteroid for "science" and not even for man, and nothing I can say about "her" any longer has to do, bears any resemblance with what she is.

Diplopic, the poem takes in that moment of loss of credence in the figurative moon. That is sense and it makes no sense. The separative power of the poetic view widens the gap.

When of a thing whose name I hear, I say that it's not about it but about another, for example "not about *this* life, but the other," I set my sights on its other in a one and the same: I dismantle, double, the other from the same. I allegorize, I invent the allegory.

The same
beside itself
besides

In the consequence of your *discessio* here are some quotes from published poems to read over again.

"Backwards, backwards,"[14] since the decease, in the faint backlight, by night light, a reunderstanding is arranged like a prophecy that was part of them and whose realization reinterprets them: *Forty...!*[15]

Noah's vellum sex
The gnawed animals in Lorenz's books
Here are the names Forty Eons of Tears on the Iris
And you haven't seen anything yet and the persecution[16]

And this, in the same book from youth, even more terrible:

With frankness what are you who you what what
Haste that all be done be done poorly face[17]

Or:

That dead woman, such a likeness, to whom we can say everything
You dead beloved killed kill departed yonder so close
She reclaimed her words buried in herself[18]

Or, in *Recumbents*:

"I am going to die, farewell," so ran the woman's silhouette youthful
from behind in the film, caught-up-with stopped a second by the hand of
swelling music, but ripping herself away toward the death she is fleeing. I
went before you, escort me!
"No! Do not leave us! Do not fall into the outer abyss..."
Several went down to the underworld grasping roots on the slope of
the voice, comploring she-who-disappears, who is ravished, here is the
song they heard, a brakestorm: the threnody celebrated the dilation of the
moment of death it was playing back in slow motion. Which horror? The
horror of that single lapse of not returning. The requiem repeated that rise
of stupor in the unshareable, shared by those dying and we the pomp *who*
hold them back, accompany them, turn them away from death.[19]

Farewell to friends made in these last few years. We'll see each other less and less. You were her friends and thus mine. We shared the fear. And the memory that we share returns to tacitness, gaining in silence, and shared with increasing inequality, since her share will grow in me, become relative in you, will be what, linking us, defers our seeing each other, "preserving these things in our hearts."

I can no longer take Avenue René-Coty which leads up to the Cité Universitaire, towards the "palliative care" ward, I can no longer take it without going back up towards the corridor of that death; crying. I can no longer take it.

Our last two nights, at the extreme. You in the hospital bed, in the Cité Universitaire, on the eighth floor, the one for special care, where the room's doors are left open, and there are potted plants and classical music, you my dear stretched out in a coma, I'll no longer see your eyes, your weightless body has returned to its skeleton, the small mass of the tumor like a lump in the lower right jaw and on the maxillary; the sickness has sealed your mouth; for two days and two nights your life is holding its breath: suspended and taken back, a silence and something like a weak inverted sneeze, a long silent flat spot without exchange, then the final instant, that sudden inhalation, at the extreme, a hiccup, and the regular repetition of that terrible trochee in the night,

me to your left as I was throughout our life, slightly below on the cot, under the level of your agony, my ear open like an eye, without thoughts, losing consciousness or all ears,

our last two nights as spouses, our final conjugal bed, our last side-by-side recumbence before death.

What is is a something-someone relationship; for example, right at this moment Monique and this room where she *is*, in the "world" very elsewhere very close—which is for and by her. Thus, there is "world." A relationship such that there is never an in-itself on one side nor a *solus ipse* on the other that would come together and meet: these are two abstractions of the subject. The relationship is strong, it's "transcendental." And this relationship is always, at the same time, for a third party—for example here, for myself who speaks of it; relationship to a relationship, for an alter ego. Ego is always, at the same time an alter, a self that thinks there and thus thousands of relative relationships are interwoven; that with which the novel grapples.

To be born, to exist is to inexist for thousands of our contemporaries. "You don't exist."

However, the deceased one is dissipated much more quickly and more exclusively than I, while not believing in much of anything, thought. *To lose* someone very close is to be caught up in this "incredible" experience of dissipation, like some laboratory or science fiction Cosine that might set off the annihilator by mistake and vaporize some substance. "Hey, wasn't someone or something right here before…?" "No, nothing…"

Placed into disappearance the departed, effaced by the among-the-living; the rows have tightened, still the same spaciousness, the same full void… You miss a single being and nothing is depopulated. Viduities.

Fellini's little "pebble" in *La Strada*.

In *this* place, to be sure, "I" am "irreplaceable"—by position, but without subjectivity; discernible: numerically. One more, one more—this simply means that there's room, next door, and in between, and no need to upset either the will or the love of God for "me." The not-wanting-(to-be-in-)another place than this one, belief in the fatum and fear of any exchange of destiny (one never knows), that makes up the "I" position, makes no appeal to "God."

The so-called "horizon structure"[20] causes things to differentiate when brought together. Thus bringing together, in the sense of poetic art, results not in conciliatory assimilation, but alteration. Upon approach, the thrill of a metamorphosis...

You're there you'll no longer be.
You'll soon no longer be there you already aren't
Take yourself away. Time becomes cosmic
You're still there. We'll soon no longer be
Nobody left. This will have been
make as if we were there as if we were no longer there.

Yet the king's second body in those days (or the first) was not a body of today's magazines, but a stinking, obese, gangrened body, a normal, exposed one like all the others, a true body. The most common. Royalty was "incarnated" in it.

I recover this phrase in a notebook from before the last operation in the hospital:
She's going to be laid out, torn apart, savagely, as if by loosed dogs.
Returning to animality—to be able to die like an animal

Dissymetry in no way prevents reciprocity.

The doctors surprised me. None of those who played an important role in what was not a cure but incurability and dying [*morition*]—I'm not speaking of friends from our life who were also doctors, but of doctors who, without becoming friends, cared for her, accompanied her from threshold to threshold downwards near the end for 30 years or 5 years or the last two years, not only none was present at the funeral, which is natural, or in any other manner outside their service, but none will have addressed a word in memory, a line of sympathy, not one line. And I realize it's quasi deontological, and I realize that the dying [*le mourir*] of others, close and less so, constitutes their daily escort, and condolence in the etymological sense their atmosphere, and that it's a matter of not batting an eye, and I realize that anxiousness is their company... I know, but still.

No solution. Death alone serves as a way out. The problem disappears—dissolved rather than resolved. And afterwards? New aporias. That's all. And death.

There was a discussion among the pronouns in order to find out if it would be I or he, him or me, and she or you, to you or to us, who would speak here. The introduction billed it as a fictitious subject of autobiography.

An artifact, the book, for example, makes its appearance. Produced and not engendered. It spreads, gains ground. So everything becomes like a book; general comparator.

In what respect had the invention of the artifact been "poetic" while at the same time technical and banausic, and ex-libris before being in the text, and thus "bookish"?

I return to that form of forgetting expressed by (the) Lethe, that river in which one immerses oneself constantly, to the Greek *lanthanesthaï*, a powerful auxiliary that affects all action-or-passion with a not-noticing. To die without noticing it, as Plato says: that's our condition. "Lethal," lethargic structure, more powerful than Sartrean *bad faith* which would be a kind of overly psychological, overly moral offspring—striving, we recall, to escape a Freudian use of the unconscious, that overly topical instance, overly fatal for freedom. This "lethargy": neither loss of memory, nor radical amnesia; it is the existential disposition that in man responds to the Law, to the double command, by the impossibility of facing the double bind; by means of an inability to do otherwise than to sidestep, conceal, answering questions *unilaterally*, *one by one*.

Now, the double bind slips into an inkling [*entente*] of and the answer to any "truth," if it be true that the latter, twice true, undoubles, unmultiplies itself on two levels and that this double or multiple meaning is what poetry strives to have understood [*entendre*] in all places, perhaps in all of those expressions making signs toward our intrinsically *thwarted* condition...

This is why the modern, "resolutely modern" injunction of Brecht, taken up by Benjamin, to *erase traces* in order to "survive culture" (an all-too-deeply cultivated iconoclasty) misunderstands deep Lethe, that river like the sleeping genius of earth in Purcell's *King Arthur*, in which a lethargy allowing one to live is condensed, and from which lucidity may splash up like an underwater swimmer resurfacing or Valéry responding to the question "What do you desire?" by "To be awake!" Why and with what postmodern amphetamine can this river be replaced? Would its drying up not be the very end of the *subject*, torn from his immemorials, from his opaque and deep *by-heart*, and thus too simplified, too obedient, amnesiac or brutal?

Poetry, "the Withheld One" (Hölderlin)[21], the esoteric, plunges into Lethe and emerges from Lethe oracularly; leads back to Lethe and tears herself from Lethe—sublimely.

Law of lethargy: I must forget my dying [*morition*], live as a non-mortal—in order to be mortal. The know-nothing-about-it, Lethe, is required. "It's [our] lethargy…" of course! If the very destiny of Being, says the philosopher, is to hide in its epoch and get itself forgotten.

Somber is life and I don't know
One dreams oneself girdled in nothingness
& thus forgotten by death
The soul is immortal; but
Is annihilated with the body that dies
Nothingness is stronger than being.

The astrophysical auction of billions (do I hear a higher bid? another?) (song of the imperceptible unimaginable inconceivable) "in" a present reduced to an orderly's vigilance, without past or future, present of that which is correlated to an expectation expecting nothing, expectant about "everything"…

I refused to see myself, erasing the mirrors, fleeing reflections, burying my ostrich head in the day-sheets.

Not "this is not representable" (for it is), but "it isn't presentable," it's unpresentable, impossible to consider together *while in society*. Thus, what we've seen, heard and, as we say, "lived" will not have been photographable, mappable. Those instants cannot be projected onto a surface, transformed into a *vista*, be exposed. There is no pornography of agony. Horror is not sublime either, for the sublime is still linked to the beautiful.

Outliving you isn't easy.

Living this outliving: a task, a strangeness, a fluke, a motif, a stupor, a remorse, an injustice, a meditation, a disproportion, a duty according to some, an adjournment, a preoccupation.

Being dislocated like an injured shoulder, the pain reset–day by day; the relation–to be invented, in order to link, in the *out-*, yesterday's living and life deserted: the stoicism of suicide at the end of the calendar.

I believe in no afterlife beyond that which is mine, today, and whose pain resumes upon waking: tenuous metempsychosis that transmits and translates from your departed life into mine what was your pain into mine like a grief transfusion.

I believe in no commerce with the dead except the one I entertain with your imprint in me, this foreign soul that "lives in me," this other truth that "dwells in the inner man," slaking the ego and that made it hospitable to alterity.

I believe in no eternal life: nowhere will we ever be reunited and sadness consists precisely in this sunken future that no work of mourning can fill, *this* sadness that will disappear, in turn, with "me." Yet these fathomless days of sadness, whose pages lined with paper simulate some perspective, are the "future life" into which your forgetting accompanies me: interminable briefness transformed into brief infinity instantiates eternity.

BIRTHDAYS

1, 2, 3, 4, 5, 6, 7, 8, 9, 10, 11, 12, 13, 14, 15, 16, 17, 18, 19, 20, 21, 22, 23, 24, 25, 26, 27, 28, 29, 30, 31, 32, 33, 34, 35, 36, 37, 38, 39, 40, 41, 42, 43, 44, 45, 46, 47, 48, 49, 50, 51, 52, 53, 54, 55, 56, 57, 58, 59, 60.

They just placed this where an explosive suicide (that which was most secret exploded where it's very public, like an unpredictable collision) happened to commemorate the place become cenotaph: "A just one found peace again," and while I understand this piety and its conventional inscription, here the funerary rhetoric troubles me, for it is no less true to write that none is just and that the deceased is not an appeased sleeper and that the living pay too dearly this extenuated euphemization of death.

Nothing in what awaits us in life after death—thus: after the beloved's death, that of the *alter ego*, one's "better half"—nothing that would authorize talking about a second life, about another life than the preceding one, where the same failure resumes, desolate, distraught: it's the *in vain* of Ecclesiastes, aridness after the mountain pass, made of hopes and disappointments, affable, to be transformed into wisdom.

"To get used to it" is the vernacular injunction, with its tight laconism. Get used to what? To the condition of mortal, unknown, ephemeral, uncertain. Ignoble, brief, invisible, insignificant, insane. With which one must make do—producing humor, conviviality, hospitality, tolerance, peace—the "illusion of joy." What machinery!

Yet another short trip. I return from Lisbon or Berlin. Can one still speak of trips? About my variation on the theme of *the cultural*, I shall not speak here—but elsewhere. But about myself, if I have failed, once again "passing unnoticed," it's quite describable, even explainable, if not comprehensible, never appearing except as endangered species. And it's not a question of resentment. My imperceptibility is due to physical characteristics upon which I do not wish to dwell: a lack of sex appeal, one might have said one or two generations ago, that senescence does nothing to help. This portrait should be undertaken by someone else—or if self-portraiture could achieve it, it would be by a process of collage and montage that would leave the job of inference to the reader.

Emotion (this alarm, this verge of tears) brushing at the cornea, at "the spectacle, ordinary as it may be" (Baudelaire[22]), even at the street, the books, at each gap in the schedule.

The play of absence-presence has changed, complexly. I have to admit that the solitude in your definitive absence into which I am retreating is sweeter to me than going out where you are forgotten, unknown, or hushed, out there where you must not be referred to, out there where you are foreclosed. The space of your foreclosure makes me hate. I would prefer— and I shall go there— the oceanic milieu, that of the desert or mountain, where humanity should never have spread, where the principle of anthropy changed death into another death, that of pursuit and destruction, and the inspection of Moby Dick into the slaughtering of whales, and the nomadic apposition of tribes and bison into massacres under the new law of the terrible OR ("it's either us or them") that causes every last one to perish, and now it is clear that I prefer the growth of great white cetaceans to superhumanization.

The emptied clepsydra divides up the void
Prayer beads. Sorting. Backgammon. Abacus.
Splendor retreats into heavens
Disproportion growing with age
All that is detaches itself; but not being, final attachment.
I make a tetrameter:
Oh my children I'd like to live closer to you
Of all the peaces that have been made and that are made we can
say: Why so late, since it was necessary.
So: now?

Phôs. Light. Photographs. Lights from a neighboring world that sweep by. Photos retrieved, flipped through, reviewed. "Mirror, mirror! Tell me what was, the most beautiful, instant of the past, what will have been, the last summer."

On the use of photos; of the album; of the precious magic mirror. The Australian one on my desk; *vita antiqua.*

Next to Piero di Cosimo, near my desk and one might say, inversely, here is Daphne transformed into a woman. And Apollo? Become amateur photographer and excluded from the scene, he replays upside down and in slow motion, the mutation that deprived him…

It's the blazing bush with big flakes of our day and the human figure trembles there without oracle. For yet "interpreting" what might happen, we still have the option of going back against the current through the metamorphoses: weakened tortures of a Hades who got earth back in a deal, Zeus ousted…

And the chance in a photo: without this decision of a certain light in the midst of the Australian bush (we are a thousand kilometers from Perth) and since in that direction the trail projected a yellow runner beneath the parallel and indifferent cumulus clouds floating above us like a Gospel truth dispensing drought upon the humble and the great I shall not have seen the kettle of laurel (it's not a laurel but I'm reading in our language) with massive floral bubblings nor all this sister earth stick-stirring [le tout des tiges tournant cette tourière de terre]. One of the figures of fortune that the years deal us: I often find it in my deal and redo the reading all the more freely for its not being a text but a temple of the mute visible cut out by the camera as tarot.[23]

Light under the horizon of the neighboring world which passes
Reascends toward the night actress eye-ringed Vega
Like Yvette Guibert or the eyelashes of a Degas[24]

Love, the fact of suddenly *being loved.* Passivity is not passive. To be desired "for what you are" is good, in the sense of good-for (the Greek *areté*); individualizing Love coming on in the passive voice instigates a use of "I" that emancipates, "causes one to leave father and mother," leave infancy.

Even Narcissus shivers at sensing himself brushed, and says "I". He almost entered into reciprocity, almost became grammatical agent, he through whom the other would have been as beloved, almost returning the favor that he just received.

They were from Thespies, Narcissus, son of Liriope, the blue nymph that the Cephissus river disrobed for her bath, swept away, penetrated. Narcissus knew that he'd die young, from self-contemplation, because Tiresias had predicted longevity for him "on condition that he never look at himself." Now, no one looks at himself; to see oneself is impossible—for he who might succeed, might as well say die.

What he saw was the covetousness of others with regard to his image. Capturing his image (the words of Freud, translated), others were subjected to that. He, on the other hand, veiled reflective surfaces, had no eye for the idol in the pupil of others, didn't allow himself so much as a look.

His twin, his sister, Echo, loved him: "I love you. I love you." "You love me? You love me?" The same. Children's games that sometimes change to furor: when each answers with the last syllables of the other, they draw each other's blood like the transsexual couple in Baudelaire's *Duellum*, "appalled by love" and "clutching each other spitefully."

Thus, avoiding mirrors, he buried his face in leaves or sand, losing the visible wherein all reverberates.

His adulating parents only encouraged his luxurious idleness. Models—often homosexual—were habitués of the bars that he'd hang out in at night. He was their model. One of them, Ameinias, who desired him persuaded him to pose for a male fashion magazine.

Narcissus knew neither how to paint nor to draw. He was a failure at self-portraiture (Dürer, Rembrandt, Chardin…), that laborious triangulation in which he might have learned to transport his reflection from the mirror's silvering to the canvas or to kneed clay into his own image, creating himself. Ameinias photographed him or gave him a time-lapse camera, taught him the art of antefixa.[25] He hated himself in slow-motion.

Or, alternately, to the contrary, intoxicated by self-recognition, seeking a provenance for this desired "image," he blinded himself by dint of facing himself down in the mirror. Take away that face that I may see! Closer and closer, eying himself covetously, reabsorbing himself, he would sometimes faint. Would he break through the enclosure by "passing through the mirror" as the possibility is claimed by some fables?

The enigma of Tiresias remains for coming directly under one's own sight is as impossible as intuition of self for philosophers. But losing sight of the icon of one's double is impossible. The privilege of vitreous resemblance clings to Narcissus's skin. Images swift as the glance or stable like paintings hem him in all the way to the cemetery. Growing old on a wake of photographs is the commonest destiny: death pins one of them to the tombstone.

Is it really the memory of that superficial face that I hated just this instant in the psyche glass that I'll miss a year from now … that effigy eroded by mysterious tricks and turns?

Why is this taste for living so keen? Probably not so much because of *sensation*, since everyone would accept totally handicapped survival provided that it be provided with sight, that one be able to observe, immortality reduced to a "living eye." A thinking "I," then. One that is curious, theoretical, waiting to "understand"… What? The secret. Of what?

Being is keen on this outlook: even though nothingness is no more than "my" extinction, itself unapparent, it panics us… Mystery! Why is being so keen on "me"? On a being, that is. Detachment detaches precisely from this. To live, from that moment, for that pure moment of deliverance, detachment's insurrection as if there were no tomorrow.

"Nothing at all"…

One meaning of the expression: nothing out of the "all" any longer emerges or reaches. Fall of metonymy; symbolization severed.

Before the supernatural, before God, the correlate of *belief* is that which is natural.

The "believer" taken absolutely, now: the believer is he who desires *just a bit more* coherence, meaning, hope … a bit more than there is! For there's *almost enough* … almost enough to believe that things will get better. —What, everything? The *just-a-bit-more*: sounds like one of Jankélévitch's notions! Almost, just about, very nearly; yes, always; and I was very nearly happy, ingenious, immortal; we'll do better next time… Generally speaking, it's as if every "individual" situation were modeled after the drowning victim almost but not quite grabbing the edge; he came this close; his last and vain attempt to save himself *would not have been* in vain *if* … and the current sweeps him away and the great fluid gravestone covers him. "Failed, we all are": now there's a quote by Mallarmé that's worth thinking about.

The constant and constituent want (for want of a centimeter, a drop, a year) maintains the illusion of the best of all worlds (the "end of the crisis," etc.) being ready-at-hand, generally realizable, setting belief into motion. But the scale of perfection that founds our measurements does not justify the reversal of this want (perfection wanting) into an absolute; the transfer of the want onto the ledger of the absolute, an absolute too *existent* (*entissimum*) to exist "like everyone else"; and excused for not doing so. We are always victims of the ontological argument.

The best could win out if; if "men were to unite." In other terms, it's the impossible that suddenly; impossible to envisage, to conceive truly, suddenly reemerges from behind by reason and *reasons*. What gets discovered in experience as impossible, whose illusion accompanies every failure: this is sudden, by "conversion" … *converted* into sign, premises, hopes, and because there have been "cures," the incurable starts dreaming that he'll be cured of the malady of dying.

And want becomes proof, "the proof!" The proof? One refers to meaning because there is some; want of virtue, hope, progress. Want signifies "in recess" what is most real, and "for want of anything else," the direction to adopt, "asymptotic" finality.

The voice singing and in a foreign tongue, thus twice incomprehensible—what does it say?—moves us because it figures the complaint of meaning, the desire to access meaning, like the moan of an enchanted animal begging to accede to humanity—or like us, to divinity, to "Love" or "Peace, and other gods. Meaning, which we have, serves only to figure the desire of meaning and want of meaning: art makes it. The structure of meaning is such that meaning, in its relation to significations, in its future perfect and conditional verbalizations, is that which suggests itself as greater, as intensity, the "truly" which cannot not be wanting —an analogical call, a "sublime" thrust toward a possibility of supplement, of fulfilling that sets off the belief that meaning and *belief* respond back and forth, the belief that what disappoints might not have come to lack, under other conditions. There is no "presence" of meaning.

The sphere of love is the one where mourning is mordant. The one that gathers together beings who are at *pains* to give each other up. The sphere of friendliness is the one where esteemed beings encountered, in many ways indispensable, forever non-indifferent (detached, thus, from the great, infinitely disproportionate mass-in-the-background of "humans," the hundreds of millions of them through the ages past and future), grow detached little by little, or else suddenly, thanks to a turn (one cannot know if an event of reencounter, of reconnoiter, of "re" is not, in the moment that it is lived as rediscovery, anniversary, redeparture, is not, *will not have been* the last, the covert adieu, the end), a turn in bonhomie, in habit, on account of a slight habitual concern. Those who love "us" are those who will miss us a rather long time ... Precious few, they give, they cause to exist the whole order of proximity, of paucity, of the "private," the whole giving experience of the livable, of the among-us, of the "measure of daily existence," of the core.

All of the friends went through it "sooner or later." It may happen that the spheres of love and friendship overlap, induce each other, become one for a time.

Being-for-death? No. But against; hostile, turned away, indifferent or refusing with all one's might, denying, forgetting—there's nothing in it to consent to, nothing to want take on board. No No; Don Giovanni's final "no." But scratch out, plug up, expulse. When I feel it approach, sidle up or enter my body ("My death a secret child, already forming"[26]), I tremble, I annul myself, "annihilated". Nothing can be got from it, hoped from it, counted on, expected, acquitted. We're not made for dying. Rather immortal or, rather, non mortal. Prepare oneself? Take care of it, like Jacques Brel, like so many who are dying. Bring suicide into it, choose my Styx? Or flee, behind the cape, exile exile exile... "Elsewhere," with the wise, on the Indian slopes? "There's something Indian about the earth." I remember, on TV, the Jainite ascetic, totally nude, climbing, along with the rest of the crowd, among the clothed, all mixed together, indifferent, fraternal, up toward the great male idol for the feast, every seven years. Mute, naïve, a widower. But pious, idolatrous, superstitious, up to the Colossus sprayed in red. That symbiosis of asceticism and idolatry is not our wisdom, our philosophy. Not for us.

Common knowledge: we know everything and we know that all of us know everything. But it doesn't change a thing.

The subject subjects himself; he must become the slave of his servitude (in the legal sense of that which constrains him by common law). I become the slave of constitutive infirmity. I, myself, am the slave of such-or-such servitude (which I don't specify here because my "portrait" only interests a few close friends, whereas the condition of portrait is general[27]): I know it and that they know it and that they know that I know they know. *Common knowledge* produces the secret, that is, the non-professable. "We all knew, but no one talked about it": the principle of the novel, that is, of the revelation of that which all know.

They thus believe themselves responsible for what is not of their doing. They call it destiny, and "my destiny." The Stoic lesson that spread was that I must answer for what is of my doing. But common superstition credits someone or another for one's beauty or birth. "He thinks he's something": strange idiotism. He thinks he's responsible for his body, which is in no way his creation. And opinion approves. To cease believing it would have dire consequences: a sort of generalized, dangerous miscreance would smile at every occasion; everywhere saluted, chance would become an idol and gaming a cult.

The I and the self and their bodies are disjoined, poorly articulated or, let's say, articulated in such a way that, as living beings, "failed, we all are." Naked man excuses himself for being such; *shame*, or that type of feeling; as if we were *incarnated* in the manner of a god (or metempsychosized as punishment, like a pariah), and *might have had the choice* had a destiny or demon not trapped us. As if Something Else were possible or just about was. But this air of "Something Else" that passes in no way stands as proof that we are not, simply, *natural*...

Do I not recognize this sorrow? Strangled softly by a friendly hand, from the inside, at the base of the neck, as it has happened, when?, so often, and now, as soon as I shut the door, cloistered, thinking of you, of her in your place, of this unemployed *tu*, of this personless personification, it's raining, what was it about?, don't I recognize it?, a slight burning that goes down like an invisible drink or as if the air were tear gas, a belt of muscles tightens in a series of jolts.

It was when a quarrel, yet more than a quarrel, had exhausted, separated us, *Duellum*, and, truly irreconcilable, we had pushed away from one another, distanced without term, each clearing away his and her corner of the world, next to the world, and I was already alone as if it were forever, and wounded quibbler of a false forever, absence rushed in as to a river mouth, a sea that would then be closed off beyond the horizon, there would come a day and a place of disillusionment, when our hands once again would embrace a cask of happiness.

She possessed exceptional "authenticity," honesty: her "I"—subject for enunciation, pronoun delegated for something else—, her body and her word represented each other well, were each other's vicar, fulfilled each other. The "first person" did not usurp *what was her "mine"*; the idiotic self didn't preempt every sentence. A body without obesity assured the linkage.

The reversibility of a setback "for one" and an obverse for-the-other, the for-me and the for-you side in communication with each other.

Praise to the human, the mortal who takes the condition's punishment—*while dying* [*se mourant*], pronominally, in the middle voice, intransitive.

Impossible not to reflect about what I might have done with that threatened life, my life, our life, maybe we would have saved what is meant by saving time, a little time. Had I wished, to the exclusion of practically everything else, to save that life, push back death, that is; had we devoted (as is said) our time to this and nothing else, perhaps she would have lived longer, before becoming the feminine pronoun of these pages—"she." And it was true for M. and N., provided that hour after hour, clepsydra for the transfusion of time, one's time be "sacrificed," never leaving one another, spending time, one's time, our time, we might have *saved* them.

Perhaps, in the final analysis, what one saves, the substance of what one can "save" is indeed time; that savings is, definitively, that "*of time*"–"a bit of time in its pure state," nothing-to-do time, time that we don't know what to do with, no more or less mysterious than "life"; the very time that one can only waste, time that is nothing but time to waste. And perhaps what one gives when one really gives, what one is the stingiest with because it is most precious is the same thing: time, "one's time." And this is what one neither wants to nor can give.

Fables attest to it: we are *getting ready*. What we are getting ready for slips away and we willingly put our meeting off to the "beyond": "Alright, it's just us two, now!" To believe is to believe that there "must be" completion, adequation, adjustment. *Self-fulfilling thought.*[28]

Our preparations are intense. The means taken and that are at our disposal (inordinate knowledge) overshoot the "objective." Objectivity exceeds the objective. With all this experience and inheritance, "he" (you or me) could have loved more, sung more, seen more, "achieved" more. I expected—better; I was made—for something else. Excess of demand over supply, of ability over the task, of knack over destiny, of resources over the plan throws us to malediction or dissatisfaction, anger, stupor, resignation. On the lookout at the mast of the voyage, the promised land retreats—except for he who managed to deceive himself. So many fables tell of recompense for disproportionate, unpredictable waiting, favor without reference to what is deserved: in eternal night, the crow desired, and then there was light (Simone Weil admired the Eskimo myth). Many fables tell of the cowardly inanity of waiting: Kafka's peasant *could have* crossed the threshold.

Being thrust outdoors, Don Quixote was given to recognize what he sought: there is the enchanted world to be disenchanted.

In the end, the way out of illusion—the outcome of the way out—is poetic. Like Ulysses *returning* to Ithaca to recount his adventures, a Ulysses who reinterprets Circe, the Lotus-Eaters, the Sirens, and the Cyclops, the knight *will have* dispersed the monsters from his dawn.

"Icarus, that young ambitious one, plunged here /.../ He died pursuing a high adventure."[29] Youthful mystical illuminations recognize what is desired, misrecognize what is beyond hope. It's her, it's him, I love! taking the candle for the light, the finger for the moon, the shadow for the prey. But it truly is earthly experience that reveals the two terms of cross-purpose and the whole enthralling game of misadventure and misunderstanding in general: the letter and its figure! Ulysses, Quixote, the Narrator… what (for the ironic readers that *we* are, turning from beyond the end back upon lost time) is the invariable of the *Remembrance* that lasts through the illusion of anthropomorphism? Nothing will have taken place but equivocation. Novelistic lies and poetic truth.

What you seek is near, right there—and is not that. The treasure is in the field; prose's plowing, language holds things at a distance while gaining access to them: so paradox remains; the electric arc of oxymoron; high voltage, paroxysm.

In order to have got to this very moment—that of leaning out over the void, over the balcony of the voyage, of the weekend, over Sunday's prow, that of sunset, detached, loving, perennial and *courtois*—history was necessary, post-war years, inheritances, speed, papers and now, inopportune, inactivity, emptiness, Zen inclinations, over-exhaustion… got to get going again.

Desertified day, "mine" is the trillionth of "the world," by a fluke in Connecticut (Auvergne, Bohemia, Transvaal, Attica, Romagne…), its autumnal ataraxia, its red and blue edges, of maple and Atlantic, its near absence of routine—the market, marching, tastes; without ties, without regrets, nothing new, like a drawing by a serial artist, "humdrum."

To be at the very end—at the prow of a *finistère*? Off alone, at last alone, like a wandering impasse, a bit of dead-end life, a cane for the blind, an erudite Oedipus at Colonnus, a palpating, animal alveolus, a tree's phalanx of leaves pleading, pulling at its roots, harassing the wind as it blows, uprooting itself, moving off, yet another sucker, a scythe's power, at each birth yet another debt on the never-balanced ledger of being, every second another malediction, an additional Job into ingratitude, an Isaac lured by every fleece.

So, what are we getting ready for? For leaving earth; for war on meteorites, for the third one, for perpetual peace; for artificial procreation; for eugenic mastery, for the total shield.

Duellum.

The discovery of "man" as my-counterpart, my-brother, the discovery of this being that is in himself similar to, being of pure semblance or *countenance*, this discovery that is our future, if we have one, will always find validation in the last line of the first Baudelairian poem. But *The Flowers of Evil* have their dark back page and it is known how the denial of fraternity turns its execration toward the *Belgians*. In the banned piece, *Against Her Levity*, the lyrical subject dreamed of infusing his *sister* with his venom by opening new bloody *lips* on her body. The hateful venom of repetitive ink with which Baudelaire infuses his Belgian brother is composed of self-repulsion, self-hatred, of disgust at his own determinedness, "vulgarity," abjection. The Belgian predicates caricaturize the French character and this portrait that falls to him. That accent, that extended family, the confinement, the cleanliness: a poor formula for humanity, a failed formula but one made up of human ingredients, the humanoid side of humans that every *I* in itself abhors. How can one not hate the components of human nature?

To repatriate the "divine." That is: Emmaus. Translate Emmaus into phenomenology into "our" over-humanized human account: desperate anthropomorphosis, up the counterslope of the vile. Gravity and grace.

Emmaus is the fable of our glorious body—modest, respectable, being-in-the-world. That's really us. The event of this apparition is hinted at, related in the pericope, "that which comes," thanks to veneration: "revealed"; attributed to a god. If we don't treat the body as a god, if we don't think within the schema of Incarnation, we'll get Auschwitz. We got Auschwitz. You will be like gods.

Understand that before it's too late we urgently need to turn books into our soul, get all the figures into the ark, translate, tirelessly translate parables into poems, into citations for our circumstances, into interviews, into the daily ordinary, translate revelations into our languages, appropriate the divine, interpret the spirit, "super-humanize."

Let's now call it the dis-creant in the slight equivocal oscillation set off by *creare* and *creddere*, for it doesn't issue or erupt from belief all at once, but *descrescendo* — increasing, that is, in a "dis" manner. And it doesn't return half-believing to the gods half-way.

The great Maldoror machine lies beached in disbelief like a useless monster of the nineteenth century, a steamworks one might visit. Our time no longer requires so much effort. The instruments causing God's death, like those of his torture before, are "execrated" relics for visiting like beautiful Churches. What he's left and of which he was the subject are millions of sermonizers' and theologians' sentences— those of his ventriloquists who calculated and subrogated him to all utterances, which in turn were related back to his Enunciation.

As for "man," we won't bother speaking of his "courage," even if we are to assume it great; no psychology or "portrait"— even in the guise of hero, of Zarathustra— will suffice; let's not waste time speaking of his generosity, serenity, reserve, humility. All portraits have taken place, the gallery is closed. Or, rather, it's become cultural. Inform yourselves. The portrait of man as son of man is no longer to be made, no self-portrait: "modern" painting is no longer "figural."

From the being "without God" (= a-theistic), from this being without Other, the loss (of the) Absolute must be evaluated; everything brought about in terms of loss by his becoming-without-God ("abandoned," Jean-Luc Nancy might say, in "divine places"[30]). For if God doesn't exist, nothing is permitted. While if he were *living* (and not just "existing") God would be love, pardon, tolerance, and not at all "moral" but permitting everything— *"quod vis fac."* Law, ethics, reason, wisdom would then be necessary— the rigor of maintaining-oneself [*se-tenir*] in and against nothingness (Paul Celan's *"Stehen"*?).

The law's obligation replaces love's license, the arbitrariness of grace, elective privilege, the pardoning of sins, religious delirium whether in monastic solitude or in the effervescence of the multitudes. We have reason to believe that "humanity"— our history at the moment it becomes our history— is heading into an impasse and seeking a *way out* (Kafka), which is not the same thing as a *solution*. And I'm not only speaking of the fact that the wall at the end of the impasse is a *screen* before which thousands of humans (soon to be virtualized) are more fascinated than those in fetters in Plato's immense Cave. Now, we wish for *anthropomorphosis*— I don't say "progress"— to continue; and it is far from certain that adherence to myths that are more or less imbued with religiosity is the best way to cover the cost of the course.

We have been ventriloquists of *God*, made him the *subject* of *our* phrases (through the intervention of priests) (in) millions of contradictory phrases. "Silence on God" (that means cease making him speak) would be a good moratorium. God is what changes nothing about what is; a useless hypothesis. The intrinsic contrarities of God, this compossibility of incompatibles, this supposedly perfect oxymoron of all oxymorons, we ought rather make of it a plan for anthropomorphosis...

The functions of judgment devolved to "God" over the course of theological centuries ought to be instantiated— confided to human institutions taking over functions of the Deceased, institutions then hoisted up by this very fact into the slight, *relative* transcendence, "ironic and cultivated," of this legality of a community put into practice.[31]

"Skeptical" criticism comes in to dissolve all these dangerous amalgams, these mental micro-organisms, these "viruses" in the head, these "fantasmatic" creatures, these chain-reactions (yes: stereo-reactive, Pavlovized "associations," in fact...), molecules of *beliefs* whose valences might be representable in chemistry— let's call them convictions, tastes, manners, representations, idiosyncratic, automatic, presumptuous, hardened (etc.) prejudices, as described, for example, in the article on populism. Critical skepticism decomposes these micro-organisms, parasites that cause me to live. Being their analysis, it sets free. And if it happens to re-compose some, it is through deliberate abstraction, constructivist, artificialist, contractualist resolution: definition in the mathematical sense (Kant) which undoes perceptive "belief," "adherence," memberships, habits (Hume), as geometry undid the empirical point or the line so that they became elements of a syntax, a relation, and a system of possible artifacts among others, compossible and exclusive (Euclid, Riemann, Lobachevsky). And criticism is always ready to dissolve its newly reconstructed elements, to exchange its axiomatic for another, never taking its requisites for atoms. What it adheres to, it constructed; it adheres to this *as if* it were indestructible. It holds to it until further *order*.

Time will thus pass through this room where I said that the world made up a corner, salient corner of a puzzle of books with the acacia corner where, at the window, sedentary pigeons exposed to the wind make a Parisian aviary— become "my" time here in the terrible present— fascinating, dumbfounding, amnesiating, prescribed.

I no longer cry this afternoon.

"Here I am," some Claudelian character might say, a kind of panoptic searchlight over countless breakers, but one that receives rather than projects light, center of nowhere and everywhere circumference, turning gazes like full arms bringing back offerings, friendly salutes, the certainty of the existence of beings, to a helpless cell where I'd like to die before dying where, distressed like the powerless god of monotheisms, giving up, repudiated, commented upon, or that master of evangelical nuptials, I have imagined suicide.

(I'd put my slippers next to the crater and, drugged to the hilt, I'd choose cremation in a volcano.)

Your last face, thinned still, framed shoulderless by the window
in the hospital coffin, cloistered on its wounded fixed-up mouth,
laid between us on the tile floor and now beneath my eyelids like the
detached head of Madame de Montbazon when Rancé appeared
    and I cite *La Vie de Rancé* because the memory of that hallucinatory read haunts me as I lead these pages toward some sort of book.

I know ("I know very well") that if chance had it that I meet X instead of Y at some friends' house, or in a train, or on some other occasion, some other clinamen in the ocean of possibilities, my current bias or prejudice would have been different: other considerations and complicities would weigh in at the conjunctures, carrying off judgment. Indebted through memory to a common third party, that kind of host sheltering an encounter, sharing the obsession of a common view still we would be favorable to each other a priori, for example, predisposed to getting on like companions in chance.

Aleatory and *generosity* go together like circumstance and its poem: generosity thinks the relationship between chance and freedom which together make up a fate. Detached as it is, it attaches to the present of the present which might have been different and graciously grants attenuating circumstances to the circumstance— speaking the present to the present's unreal.

Oh, Cebes and Simmias
It's rather our life that wears out several souls.[32]

To That Which Ends Not would thus be my title, assembling like men transformed *under* an enormous and indeterminate threat into *counterparts* the pages written from this end.

That is the moment I imagine, its dilation, its ending-not, and the poem that slows down the poignant interest for this whole existence (ours) whose being racked by the revelation of the world ends not.

Special expectation whose agreement I sought long ago on the prow of land's end in Brittany.

> *I waited like a lover who makes a*
> *date in some field*
> *beneath a rigid apple tree and*
> *in yellowing grass waits all afternoon beneath tons of clouds. The lover*
> comes not.[33]

Or, in America:

When the afternoon sought its conclusion in Annapolis and the sky took on delight from the light, a taste of ending was suggested by this genitive— end of the end— that Annapolis' tip hadn't yet offered: that of a bay of the bay, of a loop that locks itself the bay with curled up edges where the world of travel came to an end, that still might not take place.

The afternoon was ending near Annapolis along whose edge the detour sought its return, moving along the bay with Monique and Sylvie. Straying invented an inaccessible access imagined an access, the bend in the ...[34]

Or, coming up out of the Saint-Sulpice parking garage:

> *Is this why what I like*
> *The hard-wearing the one-to-one*
> *Climbing the stair slow prone to wear*
> *With the suddenly changed kite sky tied to my wrist*
> *Climbing so close to the stair beneath the sky*
> *Where the carnivorous cloud weightlessly awaits our cadavers.[35]*

My book rereads those that came before it.

Someone was and is no longer; I attest to that existence. Was in being loved. Each of us is threatened by the same fate.

Death goes unnoticed because few die at the same time in the same place and because it occurs at the heart of private life in apartments and because the relay is immediately assured, furtive courteous transfer of words, remembrances, papers, secrets, sermons, objects that within shared knowing nurture the unspoken, the allusion, the euphemism. But imagine urban plague, massacre, earth unable to absorb the dead. Foretelling unveils mortality *apocalyptically*.

That which ends not ends
My friend my sister
You too have been alive.

I didn't have the presence of mind; some other time I'll find the turn of phrase for the place.

I don't hear your language in your foreign tongue, the things of your language. And reading me, foreigner, you don't hear the euphemy of this prose— what is sought after in the way of truths, that makes the difference between manners in which meaning goes about it.

Thomas Mann liked the fact that Chekhov supposedly said that life was like a respectable insomnia.

The abyss of the vernacular, the invincible betweenness of language and ethos, the idiomatic untranslatable, the privilege of indefeasible birth— the "land." And a slight transcendence pulls us toward a more common sense. Resemblances, exchanges, translation.

Where to act against misfortune? The moralist without borders witnesses the unending increase of his pain. One person's misfortune is the misfortune of others. The hired killer thinks he's got orders from God.

Hence there is always a dual constraint within disproportion: the utopian apex whence the two disjoined scales are disclosed together with the sight of their disproportion, and the mandate to be in *both scales at once*.

And since the Two of Disproportion are true, together, since we are nothing derisively in comparison to the inanimate hole, yet everything is worthwhile and since the least desirable thing incarnates errant value like the Knight— we have no other choice but this choice without being able to be *in the same time* at both ends. At the same time we have the duty to articulate both, to place into relation, to undertake the unification of zero and infinity in the form of its cherished diminutive in which life is nullified, gets put into proportion with its nothingness.

Syncopated attempt, "leap into the unknown," sacrifice thrust the blessed, precious share into death, "the only begotten son." Concerted execution, public, manifest, economical, it repressed massacre onto the verso of murder.

Prosopopoeia is necessary for there to be reciprocity. A face and a word must be given to that which has none or not enough. Envisage and look long and hard, give voice to this alterity whose indeterminacy may frighten. Represent and present oneself before this alterity of the other when it lacks concretion. Hypotyposis, allegory are needed— poetry. Whatever being you might be, you are not any old unfigurable thing. I recognize you, *tu quis es*, you are: face and name. We can speak, perhaps. To recognize each other will make recognition possible.

The face is that thing— the only one— that in itself, taken intransitively and absolutely, *resembles*. The face, making of semblance, of man-semblance (and affection for animals seeks their face), opens up the order of "likeness in itself," the aspect of a being which in its being is like— "my counterpart." Made through and through of likeness, it's as if he resembled; and prosopognosia— that stupefying anamnesis— delights in the simple fact of recognizing the other from light years away. The face calls forth the figure. The source of dread at all "ugliness" is perhaps horror mixed with compassion at disfigurement of the figure.

It's as if he resembles–himself in himself: this self-portrait I carry before "myself" each morning with paint, tattoos, mimicry, expressivity, mean-to-say that says that I resemble. *What?* asks attribution's disquietude. Desire desires to attribute this face that achieves some likeness to a Model, in the Image of Which.

Image is sometimes expressed as copy, sometimes as model. Before the model/likeness difference, *imitatio* radiates, promotes, separates–like the text of Genesis–the difference that will become prototype and exemplar.

In expressing, however, the face expresses nothing. Nothing other than human likeness. Whence fraternity ("one man and who is worth all of them"…) and hatred ("I don't want to see that! Not them. Not me"…)

"… is no longer."
Non-being is euphemism.

Metamorphoses into partridge, into laurel, by Assumption: that was the ardent dream of traversing death whole, unscathed, reaching the other side. But if there is no other side, no sojourn, no boat, no ferry, where will the metaphor derive its thrust?

The tragedy of the disappeared. Sacrifices surge forth, helpless, frenzied. Killings explode, endemic, stupid, aphasic. "After Auschwitz"…

Tone it down. Death is neither possibility nor escape. Less meaning. Alter the means of being-there, beginning with the more recent experience of death, disaster, deterrestration.

Not being there; being there less, insisting less; a lot less than the "absolute Self" romantically thought it should, could, might be there. Yet light, distracted, courteous, ephemeral, detached, self-effacing, passing on more and more often, withdrawn like the metaphor. Entering into a new alliance with new principles, responsibility, self-limitation, despair. All has less meaning.

The invention of scales also passes through a *definition of the indescribable* akin to the Euclidian element— point, line, plane "without thickness"...

Scales, pendulum: justice through construction requiring the invention of a point outside the world, a point that doesn't exist, a point of reference for the pendulum beneath which the earth can pass by, like at the Pantheon.

As Baudelaire always speaks the truth and it suffices that without mystery plot, without psychological gloss, without expressionism, we take literally the incipit of *The Murderer's Wine*— read without alcohol— to understand him:

My wife is dead I am free.

Free from what? Free for what?... Free, in that freedom which the two, conjointly, promised each other to give up, that they dreamed of sharing as impossibility of their condition. Free to no longer cause the harm that betrayed that promise: the strange refusal of love, refusal of incarnation, refusal of intimacy, refusal of the condition, the proximity, in exchange for chimeras.

Free to recognize, in the end, the irreparable.

What now do I hold more dearly in me than M.'s death in my heart, source?

I lean forth over it, Narcissus. The enormous tear no longer returns my reflection.

To you who in dying have given me yet another book, after having given me books while living.

The voice of the headstone setter on the phone.

How to write something on the stone? What quote to choose?—
one that wouldn't feign or mime hope or sound quivery voiced. What
phrase, lapidary, what "right" words, dare one inscribe? What sentence
to place in the balance with the other side of the marble, suitable to
counterbalance nothingness, to pierce the gravestone with no *trompe-
l'âme*? What "diminutive infinite" (Baudelaire)[36], what lever good
for adjusting sadness with the earth, for reflecting the surroundings
and the sky above, for turning thought towards the dead with piety,
for corresponding to our sorrow each time we return, for making us
unanimous, for disarming fear, refusal or the ugly expression— for
summing up?

I'll leave the stone with only the last name, the two woman's names,
and the two dates.

The trivial voice— on this side, from within, from below, from the edge, from the back, from the plane of this slope, from this verso, just short of this side. And never from beyond the grave; and there is no other side. From the foot of the embankment of the living.

Here's the marble mason's yard
A dwarf town of bombarded shops
Through the tomb with its shade mouth
One deceased enters into the center of the earth.[37]

I used to throw myself at the notebook with thoughts several times a day— which dragged on. Today, numbed, immobile at the window of one remembrance: the little cabins of worked wood on the Grand-Bassam road, with antique dealers and artisans.

– Your indifference…

– No! It's not a matter of indifference!

I'm just devastated by sorrow— a sorrow so out of proportion even with this acute mourning that it seems to take advantage of the situation to rush forth immeasurably: sorrow of Disproportion itself, the way water replaces everywhere when it rises into the least cranny, turning itself into the element that substitutes for air under our very eyes.

Seeped into and soaked by an incurable grief that is itself equivalent to or transformed into ravaging compassion, into "gift of tears," and like an upholder of the law without cause or grievance, I measure infinity in proximity, infinity *between*, the holes of nothingness in the nearness that separates the non-distant, the unsubstitutability of *sames* in a time more fractal than space.

WAKE FOR ONE BORN

A plank inclined over the salty abyss slips
the finally drowned returned to the drowning
the sailor in his chest become cenotaph
a pensive departed one sometimes sinks

this slip raises Lethe's ocean
lone diluvian river
pleroma of prophesy

They die without knowing it said Plato
And later a god: "Forgive them for they know not."
But we to
day know this
That at the instant of my death
no living being, no thing of use
counts on you any longer
on your having been born   your no longer being

And all during the Wake
Wake des Geborene
are already drunk on happiness

STORY OF TEARS

My lacedaemonian fox
My vulture at the liver
My kingdom divided against itself
The enemy is before us

Love does not cognize
but recognizes
like the witness
Tears attest to it
The spring from which they arise
in Mycenae in Emmaus in Paris
Neither physiology nor psychology
replenishes it
instead our incorporeal body

No one grants
The supplicant's petition
But the oration without vocative
Pursues the inexorable   in vain

For full bibliographic information on works by Michel Deguy, that are mentioned here by their titles only, see Hélène Volat's on-line bibliography at http://hvolat.com/Deguy/Deguyindex.html

Endnotes

1 "ce vers que j'attribue à Camoes depuis qu'un ami le cita comme venant des *Luisades*, trop de fois murmuré, trouve son accrochage." *Desolatio.*

2 "Un homme las..." translated as "A man tired" by Clayton Eshleman in *Given Giving: Selected Poems of Michel Deguy*. Berkeley: University of California Press, 1984, p. 55. Hereafter *GG*.

3 *Tombeau de Du Bellay*, 172.

4 *Actes*, 107.

5 *Figurations*, 231-31.

6 From "Histoire des rechutes" translated as "History of Relapses" in *GG*, 133-43.

7 *Ouï dire*, 26.

8 *Wuthering Heights* has been translated into French as *Les Hauts de Hurlevent*.

9 "Far From the Madding Crowd" in *Jumelages*, 18-19.

10 Charles Baudelaire, "Duellum" translated by Richard Howard in *Les Fleurs du mal*. Boston: David R. Godine, 1982, p. 40. "Hearts ulcerated by a full-fledged passion," Anthony Hecht's attempt in [Marthiel & Jackson Mathews, eds.] introduces a confusion not present in Baudelaire's original (p. 45).

11 Not previously published.

12 "Arrête ce moment" (*Ouï dire*) translated as "Hold this moment" in *GG*, 81.

13 "Elle l'aide à passer" (*Ouï dire*) translated as "She helps him on" in *GG*, 85.

14 Guillaume Apollinaire, "Bestiaire." This is the movement of the crayfish.

15 Michel and Monique were married on September 16th 1953. Plus 40 = 1993. She dies in January 1994. "Forty" is the number of years they lived together as husband and wife. (This note was suggested to me by Wilson Baldridge.)

16 *Tombeau de Du Bellay*, 176.

17 *Ouï dire*, 88.

18 *Ouï dire*, 83.

19 "Mouvement perpetual" translated as "Perpetual Motion" by Wilson Baldridge in *Recumbents*. Middletown, Conn.: Wesleyan University Press, 2005, p. 27.

20 Cf. Edmund Husserl.

21 In the second version of "Griechenland," Hölderlin writes, "Everyday but marvelous / God has put on a garment. / And his face is withheld from the knowing / And covers the winds with art" in Michael Hamburger's translation of "Alltag aber wunderbar / Gott an hat ein Gewand. / Und Erkentnissen

verberget sich sein Angesicht / Und deket die Lüfte mit Kunst." *Poems and Fragments*, Cambridge: Cambridge University Press, 1966, pp. 564-65

22 *Fusées* §XI.

23 *Donnant donnant*, 20-21.

24 Last three lines of "L'été l'hiver la nuit la nuit" (*Figurations*) translated as "Summer Winter the Night the Night" in *GG* 123.

25 Michel Deguy confirmed that this is an allusion to *Notre Antéfixe* by Denis Roche (Paris: Flammarion, 1978). In that work, the term "antefix"— which originally designated "ornamental tiles or other work on the eaves and cornices of ancient buildings, to conceal the ends of the tiles" (*OED*)— is usurped to mean a type of automatic writing that accompanies photographs that Roche took of himself and Françoise Peyrot using the camera's delayed shutter function to commemorate the tenth anniversary of their relationship. Roche describes the process in the work's preface, "The Machines' Entrance," pp. 22-24.

26 Paul Valéry, "La Jeune Parque" translated by Alistair Elliot. Newcastle upon Tyne: Bloodaxe Books, 1997.

27 Difference slips in between two appearances: that of "my image" for the other, if otherness is the region of that which sees me as I shall never see myself, and of my image for myself, the enclosed psychic sphere that cannot be shown, that no one "shall see." [Deguy's own note from *Recumbents*]

28 In English ("self-fulfilling thinking") in the original.

29 These are lines 1 and 12 of "Icare," a sonnet by baroque poet Philippe Desportes (1546-1606).

30 Cf. Jean-Luc Nancy, *Des lieux divins*. Mauzevin: Trans-Europ-Repress, 1987; 2nd augmented edition, *Des lieux divins*, suivi de *Calcul du poète*. Mauzevin: Trans-Europ-Repress, 1997.

31 Jacques Derrida meticulously comments on this passage in "Comment nommer" translated as "How To Name" by Wilson Baldridge in *Recumbents*, 198-99. "Comment nommer" first appeared in Yves Charnet, ed. *Cahier Michel Deguy. Le poète que je cherche à être*. Paris: La Table Ronde / Belin, 1996. The version of the two paragraphs offered here is that of Wilson Baldridge.

32 *Aux heures d'affluence*, 46.

33 "Le Pommier" in *Poèmes de la Presqu'île*, 40.

34 *Donnant donnant*, 11-12.

35 *Tombeau de Du Bellay*, 201.

36 In "Mon cœur mis à nu" XXX, Charles Baudelaire writes that the "spectacle of the sea" is a "diminutive infinite." Deguy analyzes this idea in "L'infini et sa diction ou de la diérèse (Étude baudelairienne)" *Poétique* 40 (1979): 432-44 passim.

37 "Le Cimetière" in *Poèmes de la Presqu'île*, 80.

Michel Deguy is a poet and Professor Emeritus of philosophy and literature at Université de Paris VIII (Vincennes at Saint-Denis).He is past president of the Collège International de Philosophie (1989-1992), the Maison des écrivains, and the Centre International de Poésie (Marseille). Deguy is founding editor of the journal, *Po&sie* and an editorial board member of both *Critique* and *Les Temps modernes*. After the Fénéon, Max Jacob, and Mallarmé prizes for various works, Deguy received the Grand Prix de Poésie in 1989 and, for *Po&sie*, the Encyclopedia Universalis prize. Among Deguy's 21st-century books are *La Raison poétique* (2000), *Desolatio* (2007), *L'état de la désunion* (Galaade, 2010), *Poésie et écologie* (2016), *L'envergure des comparses* (2017) and *Poèmes et Tombeau pour Yves Bonnefoy* (2018).

Robert Harvey is Distinguished Professor at Stony Brook University. His research and teaching deal with twentieth- & twenty-first century literatures & philosophy, critical theory, history of ideas, relations between philosophy & literature in an ethical context, terror & surveillance. He has written extensively on Jean-François Lyotard, Jean-Paul Sartre, Marguerite Duras, Marcel Duchamp and Michel Deguy and has translated Lyotard, Deguy, Derrida, Foucault, Ricœur, and other French thinkers. Among his books are *De l'exception à la règle. USA Patriot Act* (Éditions Lignes, 2006), *Witnessness: Beckett, Dante, Levi and the Foundations of Ethics* (Continuum, 2010), and *Sharing Common Ground: A Space for Ethics* (Bloomsbury, 2017). Harvey is a past Program Director at the Collège International de Philosophie.

Made in the USA
San Bernardino, CA
11 October 2018

Made in the USA
San Bernardino, CA
11 October 2018